JOY OF SPIRITUALITY

BEYOND RELIGION

NISHANT VERMA

This book is dedicated to my mother for her selfless love.

Contents

Preface

Acknowledgments

Introduction

[1] What is Spirituality?

[2] The Importance of Spirituality

[3] Spiritual Practices

[4] Spirituality and Health

[5] Spirituality and Relationships

[6] Spirituality and Environment

[7] Spirituality and Social Justice

[8] Spirituality and Future

Preface

Spirituality is a complex aspect of human experience that has intrigued and inspired humans across cultures and generations. It encompasses a range of practices, beliefs, and values that aim to connect individuals with their inner true self, the universe, and a higher power or purpose. Spirituality has the potential to provide a sense of meaning and purpose in the mundane life. It promotes personal growth to enhance well-being and resilience.

This book is a comprehensive guide to the spirituality beyond religion, designed to offer readers with an in-depth exploration of their true self. It also offers practices, beliefs, and values, and its relationship to personal growth and relationships. It is our hope that this book will be a valuable resource for anyone seeking to deepen their spiritual practice or explore spirituality for the first time.

The book is organized into the eight chapters, each of which explores a different aspect of spirituality. Chapter one provides an overview of the meaning of spirituality, while chapter two explores the importance of spirituality in our daily life. Chapter three explores the importance of developing a spiritual practice, and the chapter four explores role of spirituality in the holistic health and well-being.

Chapter five focuses on connection between the spiritual life and the relationships, while chapter six explores the importance of spirituality in saving our environment. Chapter seven offer strategies for nurturing spiritual connections and social justice, and chapter eight examines common spiritual challenges and strategies for facing those future challenges.

Throughout this book, we draw on the insights and perspectives from a wide range of spiritual traditions and practices, including mindfulness, meditation, yoga, and tantra.

Acknowledgments

I would like to express my deepest gratitude to the supreme god, who in various forms contributed to the creation of this book.

I would also like to thank family, friends, and loved ones who have provided support and encouragement throughout my life. Their belief in me was a constant source of motivation.

I would like to thank the publisher who made this book reaching to you possible, providing valuable guidance throughout the publishing process. I am grateful to the design team for their dedication and expertise in bringing this book to life.

I would also like to extend special thanks to all my teachers, mentors, and spiritual guides who have inspired and guided on my spiritual journey. Their wisdom, insight, and compassion have been invaluable in shaping my understanding of the world and spirituality.

I would like to acknowledge all the researchers, scholars, and practitioners, who have selflessly contributed to the field of psychology and mindfulness, providing a wealth of knowledge and resources for me to draw upon in this book.

Finally, I would like to thank the readers, who have entrusted me with the task of exploring and sharing the complex subject of spirituality. I hope that this book will be a valuable resource and guide on your own spiritual journey.

Introduction

Spirituality is a word derived from the root word 'Spirit'. Spirit generally means a part of individual which is eternal. Soul is another word used in the place of spirit. Spirituality is an important aspect of human life that deals with the exploration and understanding of the self, the world, and the universe as a whole. It is an ever-evolving journey of self-discovery, inner growth, and transformation that allows people to connect with their innermost desires to find a true meaning and purpose in life, and to experience a sense of interconnectedness with the world around them.

Chapter 1: What is Spirituality?

This chapter will explore the holistic view of spirituality, including its definition, history, and the different approaches and perspectives to the spirituality. It will examine the different belief systems that exist in the world and how spirituality can be a unifying force that connects people of different faiths, cultures, and backgrounds.

Chapter 2: The Importance of Spirituality

This chapter will discuss the importance of spirituality in our daily lives, including how it can help us find meaning and purpose, cope with stress and difficult times, and experience a sense of connection and belonging. It will also examine the impact of spirituality on our physical, emotional, and mental well-being, and how it can lead to greater fulfilment.

Chapter 3: Spiritual Practices

This chapter will provide an overview of different spiritual practices and techniques, including meditation, prayers, yoga, mindfulness, and other forms of self-care. It will also explore the benefits of these practices and techniques, how they can be integrated into our busy daily lives.

Chapter 4: Spirituality and Health

This chapter will explore the relationship between spirituality and health, including how spirituality can be a powerful tool in promoting physical, emotional, and the mental well-being. It will also explore the impact of spirituality on chronic illness, stress, and other health conditions, and the role that spirituality can play in healing and faster recovery.

Chapter 5: Spirituality and Relationships

This chapter will discuss the role of spirituality in the personal relationships, how it can help develop more meaningful and fulfilling connection with others. It will also examine the impact of spirituality in our communication, empathy, and the level of compassion, and how it can help us navigate the conflicts and challenges in our relationships.

Chapter 6: Spirituality and Environment

This chapter will explore the relationship between spirituality and environment, including how spirituality can help us develop a deeper connection and appreciation for the nature. It will also examine the impact of spirituality on environmental awareness, sustainability, and the preservation of natural resources.

Chapter 7: Spirituality and Social Justice

This chapter will discuss the role of spirituality in the social justice, including how it can inspire and motivate us to work towards creating a better world for everyone. It will examine the impact of spirituality on activism, social change, and the promotion of human rights.

Chapter 8: Spirituality and Future

This chapter will explore the future of spirituality, including challenges and opportunities that lie ahead of us. It will also explore the impact of technology and globalization, and how spirituality can help us adapt to these changes.

[1] What is Spirituality?

The ultimate purpose of spirituality is the end of suffering.

- Buddha

Spirituality can be defined as a search for a deeper meaning and purpose in life, and a connection to a higher power or divine force. It is a process of self-discovery, continuous reflection and contemplation that aims to connect individuals with their inner true selves, and a higher purpose. Simply speaking, spirituality is a belief in the soul which is eternal. Spirituality is a broad and inclusive concept that can be expressed in many different ways, including the organized religion, meditation, mindfulness, and other traditional practices.

The roots of spirituality can be traced back to ancient times and are deeply rooted in all cultures and traditions. The earliest evidence of spirituality can be found in shamanic practices and indigenous religions. Those practices focused on a connection between individual and nature, and the role of spiritual masters in facilitating communication with the spiritual world. Over time, the spirituality evolved and developed into more formal religious practices, such as Christianity, Islam, and Hinduism.

Spirituality is often associated with the religion, but the two concepts are not the same. Religion is a set of organized beliefs and practices that provide a framework for spiritual expression. Spirituality is a broader concept that encompasses a range of beliefs, practices, and personal experiences that aim to connect individuals with their true selves. While religion can be a part of spiritual practice, but the spirituality is not only limited to religious beliefs or the traditional practices.

One of the main features of spirituality is its emphasis on each person's unique exploration and experiences. This may involve practices such as meditation and self-reflection, which can help individuals connect with their innermost being and gain a deeper understanding of themselves and the world around them. Another important aspect of the spirituality is its focus on the interconnectedness and unity of everything.

Many spiritual traditions emphasize the idea that everyone is connected and that everything in universe is interconnected. This perspective can help individuals to develop a sense of compassion, empathy, and concern for well-being of others, as well as a greater appreciation for the nature.

Spirituality could be approached from different perspectives, including philosophy, psychology, and religion. It can also be expressed through various practices and traditions, such as yoga, meditation, prayers, tantra, and other forms of rituals.

One of the main challenges of defining spirituality is that it is inherently subjective and personal matter. What is spiritual for one person may not be spiritual for another. However, despite these differences, spirituality has the potential to be a unifying force connecting people from different faiths and backgrounds.

We have explored the different approaches and perspectives about spirituality, including its history, philosophy, and the different beliefs that exist in the world. We have also examined how spirituality can be a unifying force that connects people of different background, and how it can provide a framework for personal transformation.

[2] The Importance of Spirituality

A human is mere animal without spirituality.

- Vedanta

Spirituality is an important aspect of human life that has been valued and practiced throughout history and across different cultures and traditions. At its core, spirituality provides an individual with a sense of meaning, purpose, and a direction in life, as well as a sense of connection and belonging to something greater than one's ego.

One of the key benefits of spirituality is its ability to help individuals cope with anxiety, difficult times, and challenges. Spiritual practices such as meditation, prayers, and mindfulness can help individuals develop resilience, emotional regulation, and a sense of calm and inner peace. In addition, spirituality can also help individuals develop a positive outlook on life, which can contribute to the greater happiness and well- being.

Spirituality can also have a profound impact on physical health. Studies have shown that the spiritual practices can help lower the blood pressure, improve immune response, and reduce the risk of chronic illnesses. In addition, spirituality can also help individuals cope with the physical pain and suffering, which promote healing and faster recovery.

Another important aspect of spirituality is its ability to foster personal growth and development. Spiritual practices such as meditation, yoga, and self-reflection can help the individuals develop greater self-awareness, empathy, and compassion for all. These qualities can also contribute to better relationships, improved communication, and a greater sense of purpose and fulfilment in life.

Spirituality can also have a very positive impact on social and environmental issues. Many spiritual masters have time and again emphasized the importance of compassion for all, social justice, and environmental sustainability.

The spiritual values can inspire individuals to work towards creating a more just, equitable, and peaceful world.

Despite its many benefits, spirituality can be challenging and requires significant effort and dedication. Developing a spiritual practice can take time and patience, and may involve overcoming obstacles such as doubt, scepticism, and cynicism. However, with commitment and perseverance, spirituality can provide an individual with a sense of meaning, purpose, and direction in life that can contribute to greater happiness, well-being, and overall personal growth.

We have explored the importance of spirituality in our lives, including its impact on physical health, personal growth and development, and facing social and environmental issues. We have also discussed some of the challenges and obstacles that individuals may encounter on their spiritual journey, and how to overcome that through the dedication, perseverance, and a commitment to the personal growth.

[3] Spiritual Practices

If you know something is good, the wisdom is practicing it.

- Socrates

Spiritual practices are the rituals that individuals engage in to cultivate and deepen their spiritual connection. There are many different spiritual practices that exist across different cultures and traditions, each with its own unique approach and meaning. In this chapter, we will explore some of the most common spiritual practices and their benefits.

Meditation: Meditation is a practice that involves focusing the mind on an object and thus calming the body. It can take many different forms, including breath awareness, mantra chanting, visualization techniques. Meditation has scientifically proved and shown to reduce stress, improve focus and attention, and promote feelings of calmness and well-being.

Yoga: Yoga is a spiritual practice that originated during ancient India. It involves different postures, breathing exercises, and meditation practices that are designed to promote physical and mental health, as well as the spiritual growth. Yoga has been shown to improve flexibility, strength, and balance, as well as reduce stress and anxiety.

Prayer: Prayer is a practice that involves communicating with a higher power or the divine presence. It can take many different forms, including reciting mantras, engaging in silent contemplation, or participating in group prayers. Prayer has been shown to promote feelings of gratitude, connection with the divine, and overall well-being.

Self-reflection: Self-reflection is the practice that involves examining one's own thoughts, feelings, and behaviours in order to gain greater insight and self-awareness. It can take many forms, including journaling or therapy. Self-reflection has been shown to promote calmness, personal growth, grater self-acceptance, and emotional regulation.

Mindfulness: Mindfulness is a practice that involves paying attention to the present moment without any judgment. It can be practiced in many different ways, including through the meditation, breathing exercises, or everyday activities such as walking or even eating. Mindfulness has been shown to reduce stress and anxiety, improves mental health, and promote feelings of calmness and well-being.

Gratitude: Gratitude is a practice that involves focusing on the positive aspects of one's life and expressing appreciation for them. It can take many different forms, including keeping a gratitude journal, expressing gratitude to others, or simply taking time to reflect on one's blessings. Gratitude has been shown to promote the positive emotions, improve relationships, and increase resilience during difficult times.

Service: Service is the practice that involves helping others selflessly and contributing to the greater good. It can also take many different forms, including volunteering, donating to charity, or by simply performing the random acts of kindness. Service has been shown to promote feelings of purpose and meaning, as well as increase social connection and empathy.

We have explored some of the most common spiritual practices and their benefits. These practices can help individuals cultivate a deeper sense of connection, purpose, and meaning in their lives, as well as promote the physical and mental health. By incorporating some of these practices into the daily routine, individuals can enhance their spiritual growth.

[4] Spirituality and Health

Health is wealth.

- Proverb

Spirituality has been associated with various health benefits, including improved mental health, reduced stress, and increased resilience. In this chapter, we will explore the relationship between spirituality and health, the different ways in which spirituality can promote well-being, and the scientific evidence supporting the benefits of spiritual practices for the physical and mental health.

Spirituality can have a significant impact on an individual's overall health and well-being. This link between spirituality and health is based on the understanding that the body, mind and soul, all are interconnected and interdependent. When an individual's soul needs are met, it can promote overall health and well-being.

Spiritual practices, such as yoga, prayers, and mindfulness can have many positive impacts on an individual's overall health. Some of these benefits include:

Reduced Anxiety: Spiritual practices can help people reduce stress and anxiety, thus promoting a sense of calmness and relaxation in the body.

Improved Mental Health: Spiritual practices can help people develop a greater sense of mental and emotional well-being, promoting positive emotions such as happiness, contentment, peace and serenity.

Increased Resilience: Spiritual practices can help individuals develop greater resilience during challenges, promoting a sense of inner strength and ability to bounce back from any adversity.

Enhanced Immune Response: Studies have shown that spiritual practices can enhance immune response, leading to a lower incidence of illnesses, infections, and diseases.

Shield Against Depression: Spiritual practices could reduce the risk of depression and all other mental health disorders by promoting a sense of meaning and purpose in life.

Improved Overall Health: Spiritual practices can have a positive impact on the overall health, leading to improved quality of life and increased lifespan due to less stress.

Spirituality has become increasingly recognized as an important aspect of the healthcare sector, many doctors now incorporating spiritual practices into their treatment plan. This recognition of spirituality in healthcare has led to the development of spiritual care services, which aim to provide spiritual support.

Spirituality is not just an individual practice, but also involve community and social connections. Spiritual communities can provide individuals with social support, a sense of belonging, and a place to explore and practice their spiritual nature. This sense of community and social connection can have significant positive impact on an individual's overall health.

Spirituality can promote overall health by addressing the connection between body, mind, and soul. Healthcare providers are increasingly recognizing the importance of spirituality in the healthcare and providing spiritual care services as well. The community and social connection also play an important role in promoting spirituality and overall health.

[5] Spirituality and Relationships

Life is a continuous dialogue between you and other.

- J. Krishnamurti

Spirituality can have a significant impact on the personal relationships, including their relationship with themselves, others, and a higher power. In this chapter, we will explore the role of spirituality in relationships, how it can enhance the quality of relationships, and the various ways in which individuals can incorporate spirituality into their relationships.

Spirituality can promote healthy and fulfilling relationships by providing individuals with a sense of meaning, purpose, and a deeper connection. It can also enhance communication, compassion and empathy, leading to positive interactions with others. Additionally, spirituality can provide individuals with a framework for understanding their place in the world and their role in relationships.

Spirituality promotes self-awareness, which allow individuals to develop a deeper understanding of their values, beliefs, and needs. This self-awareness can enhance an individual's ability to communicate needs and desires in the relationship, leading to a more satisfying and fulfilling relationships.

Compassion is an important aspect of every relationship, and spirituality can induce the development of compassion towards oneself and others. The inculcated compassion can lead to more supportive and nurturing relationships, where individuals feel heard, understood and validated.

Forgiveness is another important aspect of relationship, and spirituality can promote forgiveness by providing individuals with a framework for understanding the interconnectedness of all beings. This understanding can lead to greater empathy and understanding towards others, allowing individuals to let go of personal resentment and anger.

There are many ways in which individuals can incorporate spirituality into their relationships, including:

Practicing Gratitude: Expressing gratitude towards oneself and others can promote the feelings of connection and positivity in the relationships.

Cultivating Mindfulness: Mindfulness practices and rituals can promote greater awareness in the relationships, leading to more meaningful and authentic interactions with others.

Shared Spiritual Practices: Performing and enjoying spiritual practices with other like-minded individuals can promote a sense of connection and understanding in the relationships.

Conveying Personal Beliefs: Conveying one's core values and beliefs can promote a deeper understanding and connection with others, leading to more fulfilling relationships.

The spirituality could enhance the relationships by promoting compassion for all, self-awareness, and forgiveness. It can also provide individuals with a framework for understanding their place in the world and their role in relationships. Incorporating spirituality into relationships can lead to positive interactions, a greater understanding among individuals, and more fulfilling relationships for everyone.

[6] Spirituality and Environment

Nature is the best medicine.

- Proverb

Spirituality and environment are interconnected in numerous ways. Spirituality can bless people with a deeper connection and appreciation for the nature, leading to more sustainable and responsible environmental practices. In this chapter, we would explore relationship between spirituality and the environment and how the individuals can incorporate spirituality into their environmental practices.

Spiritual people deeply understand the interconnectedness of all things, including the environment. This understanding can lead to a greater appreciation for the nature and a strong desire to protect it. Additionally, spiritual practices such as meditation and mindfulness can promote a deeper connection with nature, leading to a sense of responsibility towards the environment.

Environmental ethics are shaped by an individual's beliefs and values, and spirituality can play a significant role in shaping these beliefs and values. Spirituality can promote a sense of responsibility towards the nature, leading to more sustainable and responsible environmental practices. Additionally, spiritual practices such as meditation and prayer can promote a deeper connection with the nature. There are many ways in which individuals can incorporate spirituality into their environmental practices, including:

Mindfulness in Nature: Mindfulness practices can promote a deeper connection with the environment, leading to a greater appreciation and sense of responsibility towards the nature.

Gratitude for Nature: Expressing gratitude toward nature can promote a deep sense of appreciation and responsibility.

Sustainable Environmental Practices: Engaging in sustainable practices, such as reducing wastage of water and conserving energy, can promote responsible environmental practices and a deeper connection with the environment around us.

Environmental Activism: Engaging in environmental activism activities can promote responsible environmental practices and a greater sense of responsibility towards the natural world.

Spirituality and environment are interconnected in numerous ways. Thus, spirituality can promote a deeper understanding of interconnectedness of everything, leading to appreciation for the nature and a desire to protect it. Incorporating spirituality into environmental practices can lead to more sustainable and responsible environmental practices.

[7] Spirituality and Social Justice

Love is the cure for all social evils.

- Bible

Spirituality and social justice are intertwined, as spirituality can inspire individuals to seek equality, fairness, and justice for all. In this chapter, we will explore relationship between spirituality and social justice, and how people can incorporate spirituality into their efforts towards creating a more just society.

Spirituality can inspire individuals to work towards the social justice by promoting values such as compassion, empathy, and the service to others. Additionally, spiritual practices such as meditation and prayer can help individuals connect with their inner true selves, leading to a greater sense of purpose and motivation to work towards social justice.

Spiritual practices can be a powerful tool in the social justice activism. Meditation, prayers, and mindfulness can provide individuals with the mental and emotional strength needed to engage in activism and resist burnout. Spirituality can also inspire individuals to work towards social justice from a place of love and compassion, rather than anger or hatred.

There are many ways in which individuals can incorporate spirituality into their social justice efforts, including:

Acts of Service: The acts of service can promote a sense of connection with others and a greater understanding of the injustice faced by the oppressed communities.

Practicing Self-care: Taking care of oneself is crucial in social justice activism, and spiritual practices such as meditation and mindfulness can be effective self-care tools.

Building Communities: The spiritual communities provide individuals with a sense of connection and support, making it easier to engage in the social justice activism.

Personal Growth: Engaging in spiritual practices can help individuals identify their own biases and privileges, leading to personal growth and a deeper understanding of the need for the social justice.

Spirituality and social justice are intertwined, as spirituality can inspire individuals to work towards a more righteous society and a better world. Incorporating spirituality into the social justice efforts can provide individuals with the emotional and mental strength needed to engage in activism and resist burnout. Additionally, spiritual practices can help individuals work towards the social justice from a place of love and compassion, which promote a more inclusive and effective movement.

[8] Spirituality and Future

There is no hope for humanity without spirituality.

- Swami Vivekanand

Spirituality can provide individuals with a sense of direction, which can be especially important when thinking about the future. In this chapter, we will explore the relationship between spirituality and future, also how individuals can use spirituality to find hope during uncertain times.

Spirituality can help individuals find meaning and hope in the face of uncertainty about the future. Spiritual practices such as meditation and prayer can help individuals cultivate a sense of inner peace, which can help them cope with stress and anxiety about the future. Additionally, spiritual beliefs can provide individuals with a sense of purpose, guiding them towards a fulfilling life path.

The issue of climate change is one that creates a great deal of anxiety and despair among people. However, spirituality can inspire individuals to take action towards mitigating the effects of climate change. Spiritual practices help individuals connect with the nature deeply and develop a sense of responsibility towards protecting the planet Earth. Additionally, spiritual beliefs that emphasize interconnectedness and compassion can inspire individuals to work towards a more sustainable future.

Advancements in the technology can create both excitement and anxiety about the future. However, spirituality can help individuals navigate the relationship between technology and future. Spiritual practices such as mindfulness and meditation can help individuals cultivate a sense of awareness about their relationship with technology, promoting intentional use.

Additionally, spiritual beliefs that emphasize human connection and empathy can inspire individuals to use technology in ways that prioritize human well-being.

The future could be intimidating, and many individuals may struggle to find meaning and purpose during uncertain times. However, spirituality can provide individuals with a sense of direction and purpose. Spiritual practices can help individuals cultivate a deeper understanding of themselves and their place in the world, leading to a sense of purpose and fulfilment.

Spirituality can provide individuals with a sense of direction and hope in the face of uncertainty. Spiritual practices such as meditation and prayer can help individuals cultivate inner peace and resilience, while spiritual beliefs can inspire individuals to work towards a sustainable and equitable future.

www.ingramcontent.com/pod-product-compliance
Lightning Source LLC
LaVergne TN
LVHW041006150826
845672LV00002B/890

* 9 7 9 8 8 9 0 0 2 0 3 2 1 *